Name _____

Write each word three times.

bat

cat

fat

hat

rat

sat

1

Unscramble the words.

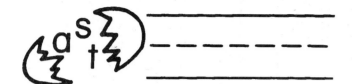 _____

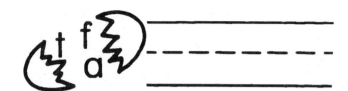 _____

 _____

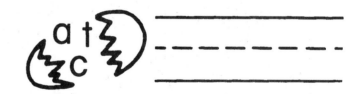 _____

_____

_____

Now draw pictures of these words.

hat	bat	rat

FS-32054 Phonics Basics

Name _____

Help Otto Octopus make words.

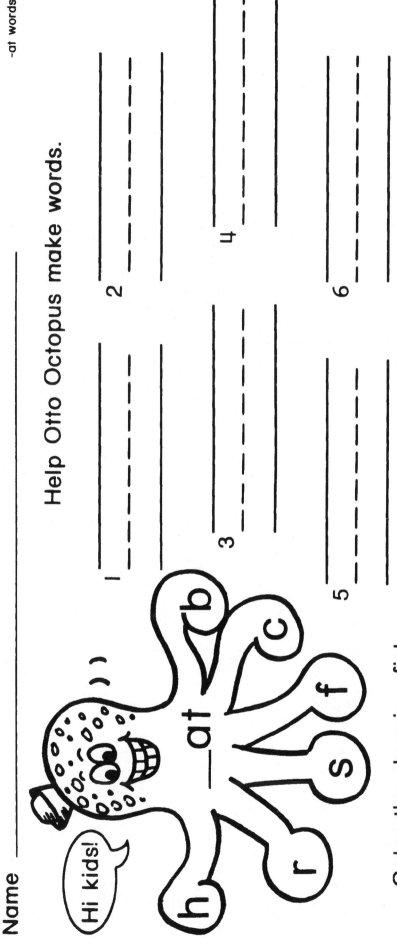

Hi kids!

1 _____

2 _____

3 _____

4 _____

5 _____

6 _____

Color the rhyming fish.

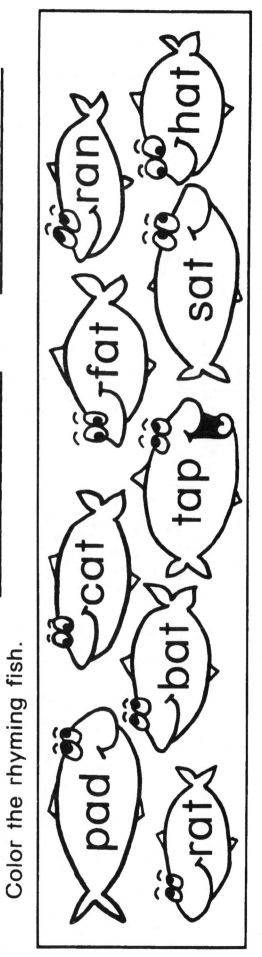

3

Find the words on Silly Sea Serpent. Write them on the lines below.

Start here

1 _____

2 _____

3 _____

4 _____

5 _____

6 _____

-at words

Name _____

Write each word three times.

can _____

fan _____

man _____

pan _____

ran _____

tan _____

5

Name _____

Unscramble the words.

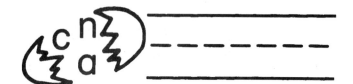 _____
_____

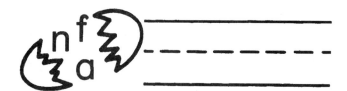 _____
_____

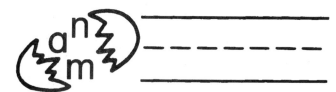 _____
_____

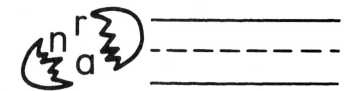 _____
_____

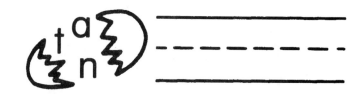 _____
_____

_____
_____

Now draw pictures of these words.

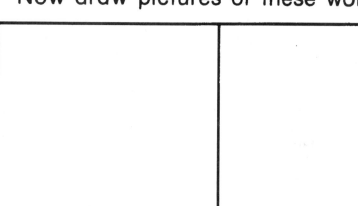

fan	man	van

6

FS-32054 Phonics Basics

Name _____

Help Otto Octopus make words.

Hi kids!

c an r t p m f

1 _____ 2 _____

3 _____ 4 _____

5 _____ 6 _____

Color the rhyming fish.

sad cap ran hat fan man pan can tan

© Frank Schaffer Publications, Inc.

FS-32054 Phonics Basics

Name _____

Find the words on Silly Sea Serpent. Write them on the lines below.

1 _____

2 _____

3 - - - - - - - - - - -

4 _____

5 _____

6 - - - - - - - - - - -

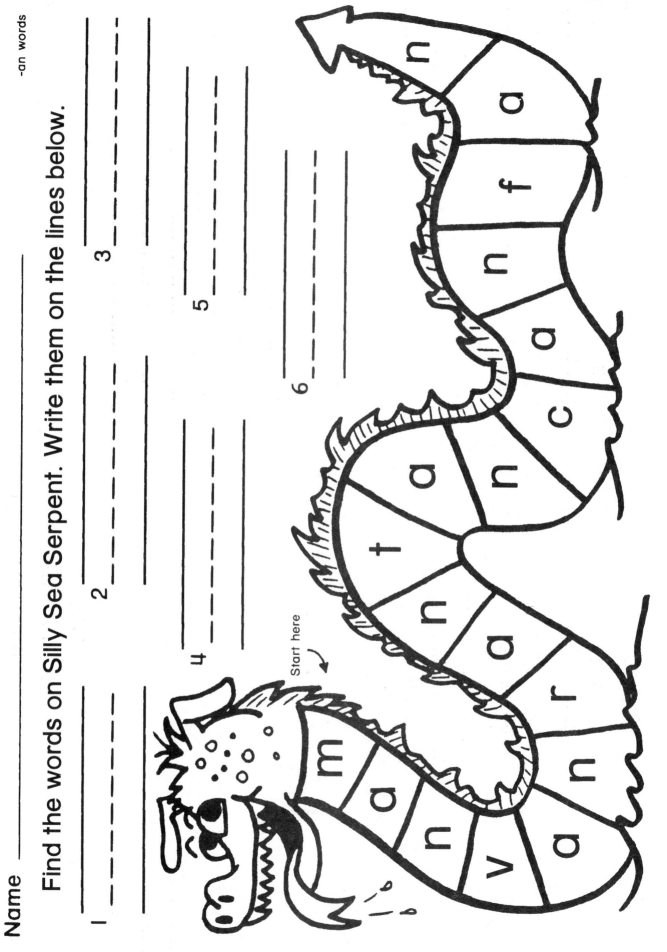

Start here

8

Name _____

Write each word three times.

-ad words

bad

dad

fad

mad

pad

sad

9

Name _____

Unscramble the spelling words.

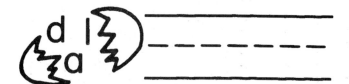 _____

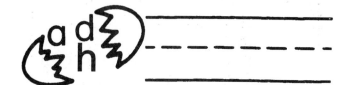 _____

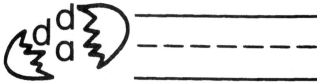 _____

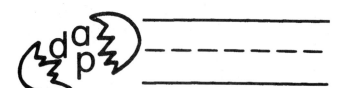 _____

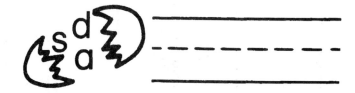 _____

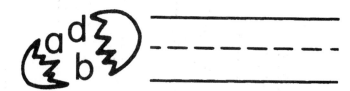 _____

Now draw pictures of these words.

| dad | pad | lad |

© Frank Schaffer Publications, Inc.

10

FS-32054 Phonics Basics

Name _____

Help Otto Octopus make words.

Hi kids!

s   m   p   l   b   d

ad

1 _____   2 _____

3 _____   4 _____

5 _____   6 _____

Color the rhyming fish.

cab   can   dad   lad   pad   bad   sad   mad   rat

11

© Frank Schaffer Publications, Inc.

FS-32054 Phonics Basics

Name _____

Find the words on Silly Sea Serpent. Write them on the lines below.

1 _____

2 _____

3 _____

4 _____

5 _____

6 _____

Start here

FS-32054 Phonics Basics

Name _____

Write the word that goes with each picture. Use the word bank.

can	fan	man	pan
bat	mad	cat	pad
hat	rat	dad	tan

Write the words you did not use here.

_____   _____   _____

- - - - - - - - -   - - - - - - - - -   - - - - - - - - -

_____   _____   _____

13

Draw the picture.

mad dad	sad man	fat rat
cat in a hat	sad lad	rat on a cat
fat man in a hat	cat in a pan	rat on a can

Name _____

Finish the word in the boat with the correct letter.
Then write the word.

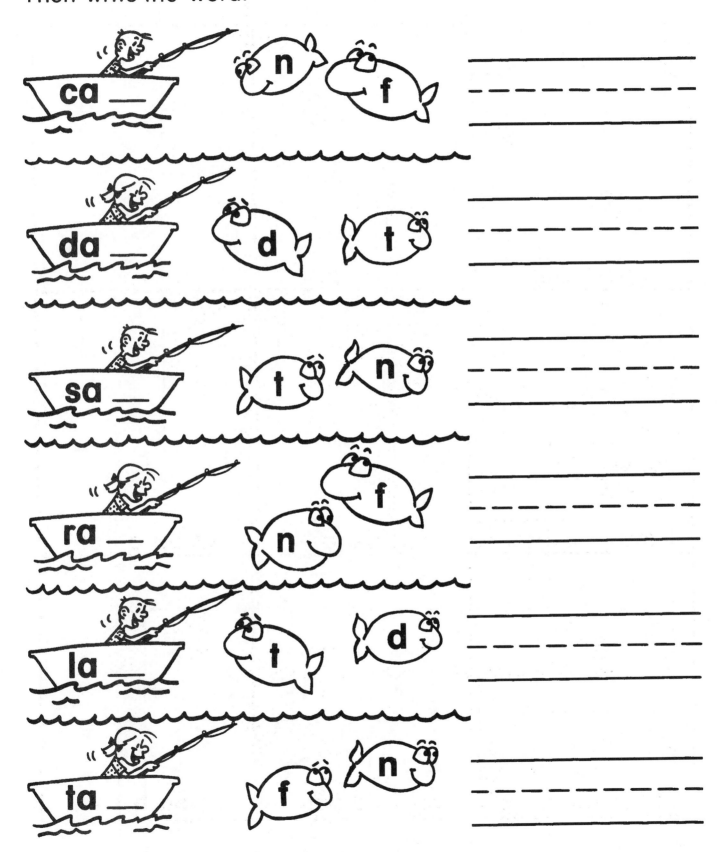

FS-32054 Phonics Basics

Choose words to put in the sentences.

The _ _ _ _ _ _ sat on the _ _ _ _ _ _ .

My _ _ _ _ _ _ has a _ _ _ _ _ _ .

The _ _ _ _ _ _ is _ _ _ _ _ _ .

The _ _ _ _ _ _ is in the _ _ _ _ _ _ .

cat	rat	fan	lad	man	pan	sad	bat

FS-32054 Phonics Basics

Name _____

Write six words that rhyme and...one more if you can!

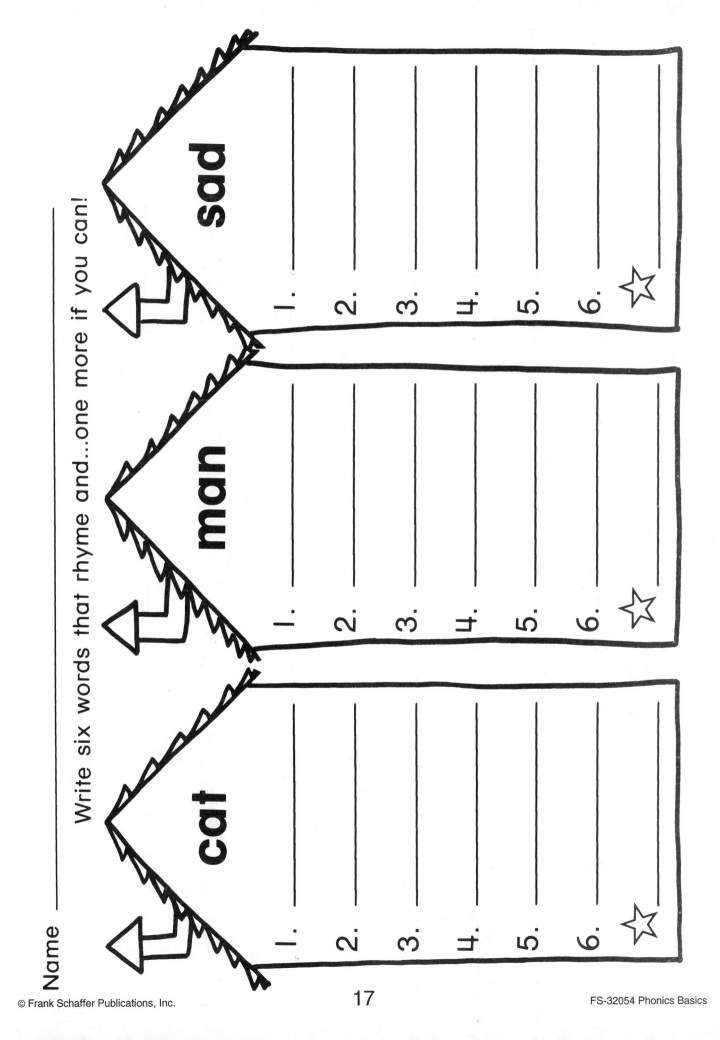

sad

1. _____
2. _____
3. _____
4. _____
5. _____
6. _____
☆

man

1. _____
2. _____
3. _____
4. _____
5. _____
6. _____
☆

cat

1. _____
2. _____
3. _____
4. _____
5. _____
6. _____
☆

FS-32054 Phonics Basics

Name _____

-ed words

Write each word three times.

bed [dashed] [blank] [blank]

fed [dashed] [blank] [blank]

led [dashed] [blank] [blank]

red [dashed] [blank] [blank]

wed [dashed] [blank] [blank]

Ted [dashed] [blank] [blank]

FS-32054 Phonics Basics

Name _____

Unscramble the words.

db
e _____

d r
e _____

e d
w _____

d e
f _____

d l
e _____

d T
e _____

Now draw pictures of these words.

fed	bed	red

19

Name _____

Help Otto Octopus make words.

1 _____

2 _____

3 _____

4 _____

5 _____

6 _____

Hi kids!

r   l   T   w   f   b

ed

Color the rhyming fish.

net   led   peg   bed   red   wed   den   Ted   fed

Name _____

Find the words on Silly Sea Serpent. Write them on the lines below.

1 _ _ _ _ _ _ _ _ _ _ _

2 _ _ _ _ _ _ _ _ _ _ _

3 _ _ _ _ _ _ _ _ _ _ _

4 _ _ _ _ _ _ _ _ _ _ _

5 _ _ _ _ _ _ _ _ _ _ _

6 _ _ _ _ _ _ _ _ _ _ _

-ed words

Start here

FS-32054 Phonics Basics

Name _____

Write each word three times.

get ____ ____ ____

jet ____ ____ ____

net ____ ____ ____

pet ____ ____ ____

set ____ ____ ____

wet ____ ____ ____

22

Unscramble the words.

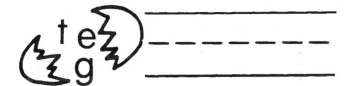 _____

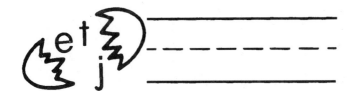 _____

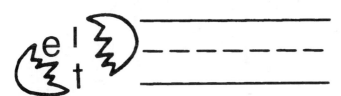 _____

 _____

 _____

Now draw pictures of these words.

jet	pet	wet

Name _____

Help Otto Octopus make words.

Hi kids!

n g s p w j

__et

1 _____

2 _____

3 _____

4 _____

5 _____

6 _____

Color the rhyming fish.

set net get leg pet wet jet bed ten

FS-32054 Phonics Basics

Name _____

Find the words on Silly Sea Serpent. Write them on the lines below.

—et words

1 _____

2 _____

3 _____

4 _____

5 _____

6 _____

Start here

t e s s t e j t e w t e g t e p e l

FS-32054 Phonics Basics

Name _____

Write each word three times.

— en words

Ben _____

den _____

hen _____

men _____

pen _____

ten _____

26

Name _____

Unscramble the words.

n h
e   _ _ _ _ _ _ _ _ _ _

e
n p   _ _ _ _ _ _ _ _ _ _

e d
n   _ _ _ _ _ _ _ _ _ _

n e
B   _ _ _ _ _ _ _ _ _ _

n
e k   _ _ _ _ _ _ _ _ _ _

n e
m   _ _ _ _ _ _ _ _ _ _

Now draw pictures of these words.

hen	pen	den

© Frank Schaffer Publications, Inc.   FS-32054 Phonics Basics

Name _____

Help Otto Octopus make words.

1 _____
2 _____
3 _____
4 _____
5 _____
6 _____

Hi kids!

_en

h   p   B   m   t   d

Color the rhyming fish.

jet   red   then   men   pen   web   Ben   den   ten

28

Name _____

Find the words on Silly Sea Serpent. Write them on the lines below.

1 _____

2 _____

3 _____

4 _____

5 _____

6 _____

—en words

Start here

FS-32054 Phonics Basics

Name _____

Write the word that goes with each picture. Use the word bank.

jet	bed	get	net
Ted	pet	hen	men
pen	ten	red	wet

Write the words you did not use here.

_____   _____   _____

- - - - - - - - - - -   - - - - - - - - - - -   - - - - - - - - - - -

_____   _____   _____

FS-32054 Phonics Basics

Draw the picture.

red pen	bed on a jet	hen in a net
wet hen	ten men	Ted and Ben
pet in a pen	ten wet men	Ben's den

FS-32054 Phonics Basics

Name _____

Finish the word in the boat with the correct letter.
Then write the word.

fe ___   d   n   _____

ne ___   n   t   _____

se ___   t   d   _____

te ___   n   t   _____

je ___   d   t   _____

ge ___   t   n   _____

32

Choose words to put in the sentences.

The ____ ____ is in a ____ ____ .

____ ____ the ____ ____ .

The ____ ____ is on the ____ ____ .

The ____ ____ is ____ ____ .

| pen | Ben | hen | fed | pet | jet | net | wet | bed |

Name _____

Write six words that rhyme and...one more if you can!

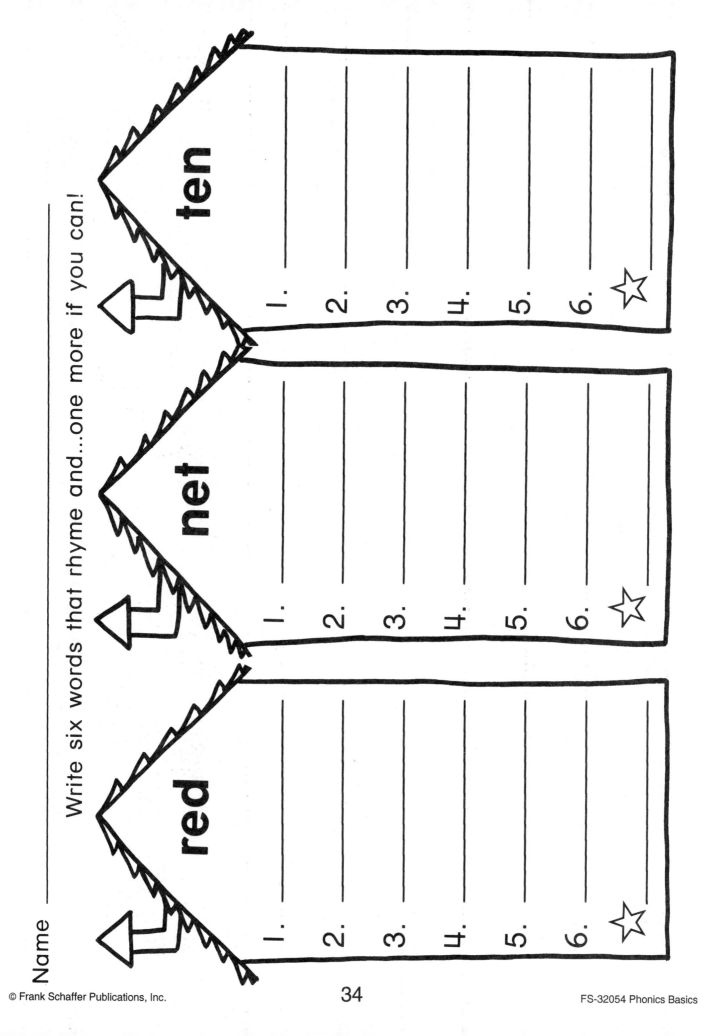

ten

1. _____
2. _____
3. _____
4. _____
5. _____
6. _____
☆ _____

net

1. _____
2. _____
3. _____
4. _____
5. _____
6. _____
☆ _____

red

1. _____
2. _____
3. _____
4. _____
5. _____
6. _____
☆ _____

FS-32054 Phonics Basics

Name _____

Write each word three times.

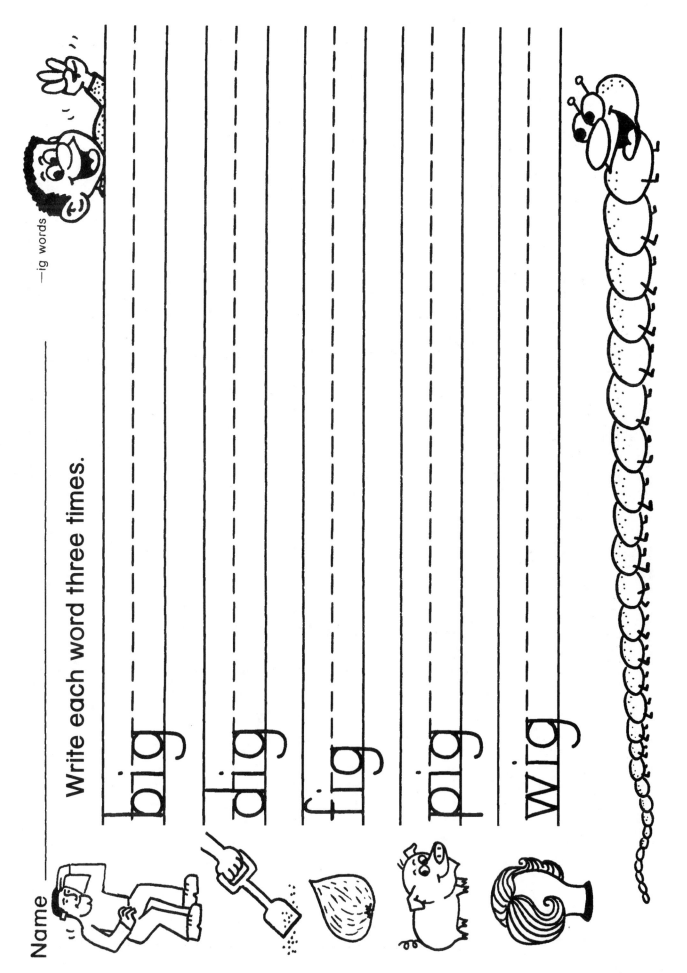

big

dig

fig

pig

wig

—ig words

35

Unscramble the words.

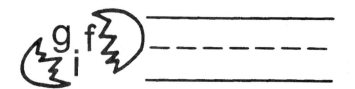

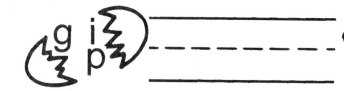

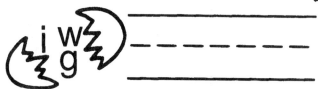

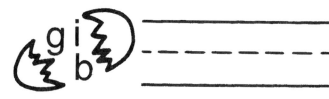

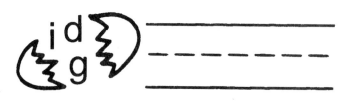

Now draw pictures of these words.

pig	wig	fig

Name _____

Help Otto Octopus make words.

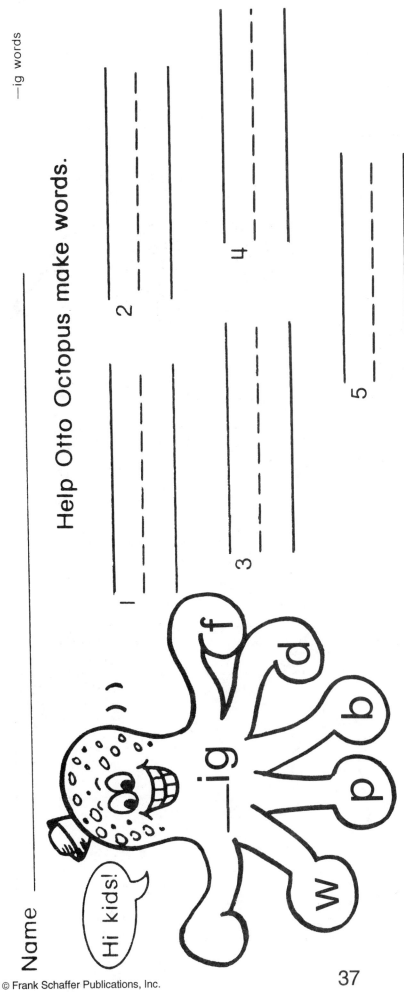

Hi kids!

f
d
b
p
w

ig

1 _____

2 _____

3 _____

4 _____

5 _____

Color the rhyming fish.

hid
fit
pin
pig
dig
fig
big
wig
tip

37

Name _____

Find the words on Silly Sea Serpent. Write them on the lines below.

1 _____

2 _____

3 _____

4 _____

5 _____

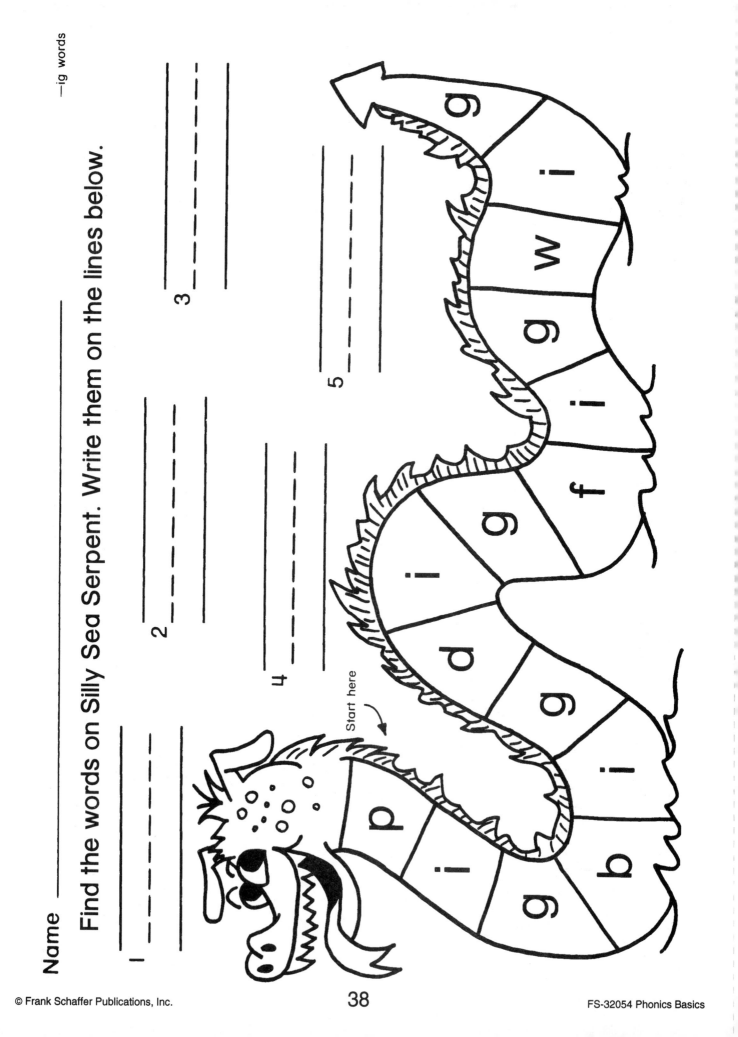

Start here

FS-32054 Phonics Basics

Name _____

Write each word three times.

dip

nip

lip

rip

sip

tip

Name _____

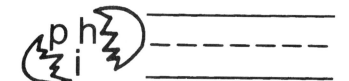 _____
_____

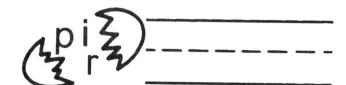 _____
_____

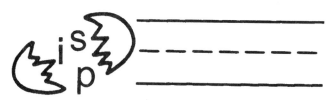 _____
_____

—ip words

Unscramble the words.

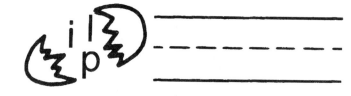 _____
_____

_____
_____

_____
_____

Now draw pictures of these words.

lip	rip	hip

Name _____

Help Otto Octopus make words.

1 _____

2 _____

3 _____

4 _____

5 _____

6 _____

Hi kids!

s r l -ip h t d

Color the rhyming fish.

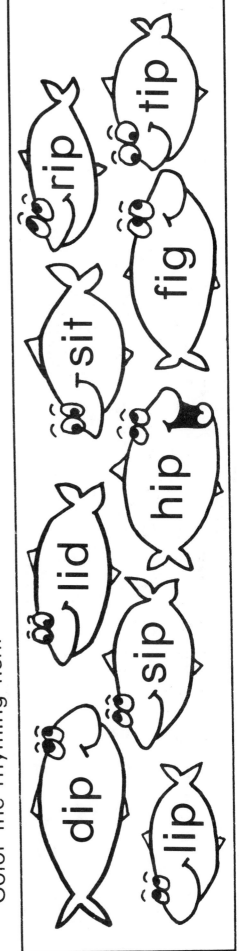

FS-32054 Phonics Basics

Find the words on Silly Sea Serpent. Write them on the lines below.

—ip words

1 _____

2 _____

3 _____

4 _____

5 _____

6 _____

Start here

42

Name _____

—it words

Write each word three times.

lit

fit

hit

sit

pit

kit

FS-32054 Phonics Basics

Name _____

Unscramble the words.

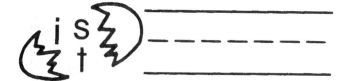 _____

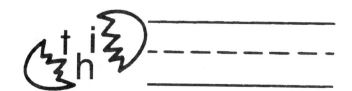 _____

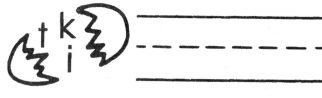 _____

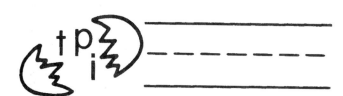 _____

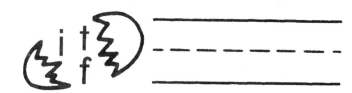 _____

Now draw pictures of these words.

kit	pit	lit

Name _____

—it words

Help Otto Octopus make words.

Hi kids!

s f p h b k

it

1 _____
2 _____
3 _____
4 _____
5 _____
6 _____

Color the rhyming fish.

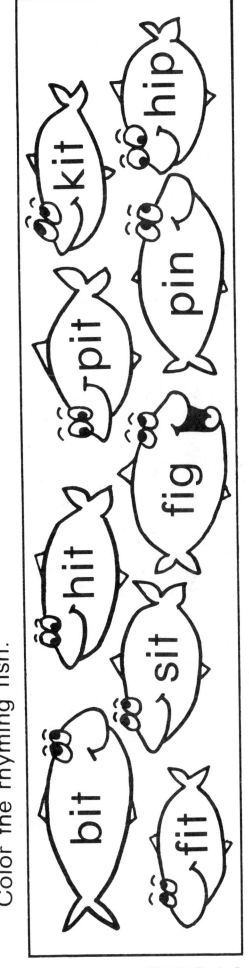

45

−it words

Find the words on Silly Sea Serpent. Write them on the lines below.

1 _____
2 _____
3 _____
4 _____
5 _____
6 _____

Start here

46

Name _____

Write the word that goes with each picture. Use the word bank.

fig	pit	big	dig
pig	wig	hip	tip
lit	hit	rip	lip

Write the words you did not use here.

_____   _____   _____

_____   _____   _____

FS-32054 Phonics Basics

Name _____

Draw the picture.

big pig	**pig with a big lip**	**pig in a pit**
pig with a fig	**Sue bit a fig.**	**pig with a wig**

FS-32054 Phonics Basics

Name _____

Finish the word in the boat with the correct letter.
Then write the word.

bi ___   p   g   _____

ri ___   t   p   _____

si ___   g   t   _____

fi ___   t   p   _____

li ___   g   p   _____

hi ___   t   g   _____

    FS-32054 Phonics Basics

Name _____

Choose words to put in the sentences.

The _ _ _ _ _ has a _ _ _ _ _.

Tim _ _ _ _ _ the _ _ _ _ _.

Sue can _ _ _ _ _ with her _ _ _ _ _.

Jim _ _ _ _ _ his _ _ _ _ _.

wig	bit	sip	fig	hit	lip	pig	hip

FS-32054 Phonics Basics

Name _____

Write six words that rhyme and...one more if you can!

sit

1. _____
2. _____
3. _____
4. _____
5. _____
6. _____
☆

hip

1. _____
2. _____
3. _____
4. _____
5. _____
6. _____
☆

pig

1. _____
2. _____
3. _____
4. _____
5. _____
6. _____
☆

FS-32054 Phonics Basics

Name _____

Write each word three times.

—op words

cop

hop

mop

pop

top

52

boing

Unscramble the words.

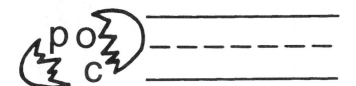

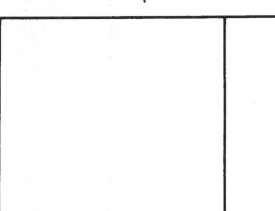
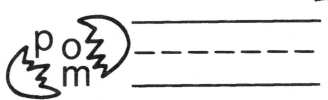
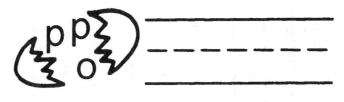

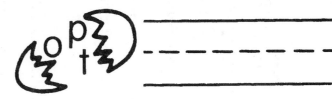

Now draw pictures of these words.

top	mop	hop

FS-32054 Phonics Basics

Name _____

Help Otto Octopus make words.

1 _____

2 _____

3 _____

4 _____

5 _____

Hi kids!

c h m p t

op

Color the rhyming fish.

sob

dot

jog

top

pop

mop

hop

nod

cop

Name _____

Find the words on Silly Sea Serpent. Write them on the lines below.

1. _ _ _ _ _ _ _ _

2. _ _ _ _ _ _ _ _

3. _ _ _ _ _ _ _ _

4. _ _ _ _ _ _ _ _

5. _ _ _ _ _ _ _ _

Start here

—op words

FS-32054 Phonics Basics

Name _____

Write each word three times.

cot _____ : _____ : _____

got _____ : _____ : _____

dot _____ : _____ : _____

hot _____ : _____ : _____

not _____ : _____ : _____

pot _____ : _____ : _____

No thanks.

56

Name _____

Unscramble the words.

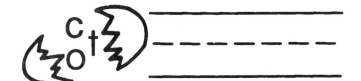 _____

_____

_____

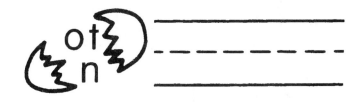

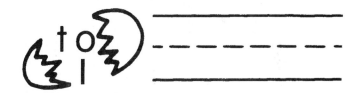

Now draw pictures of these words.

dot	cot	hot

FS-32054 Phonics Basics

Name _____

Help Otto Octopus make words.

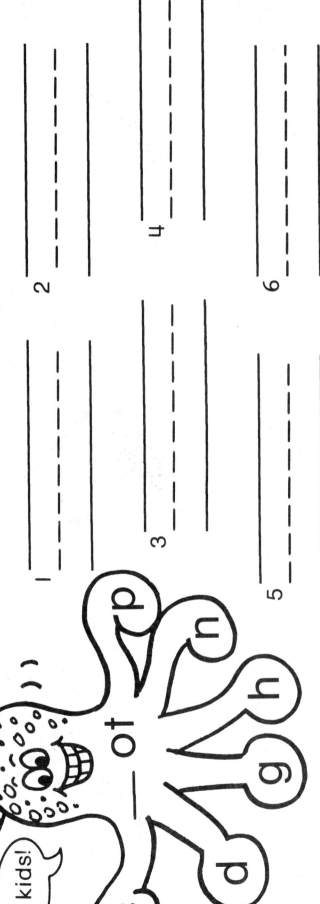

Hi kids!

1 _____
2 _____
3 _____
4 _____
5 _____
6 _____

Color the rhyming fish.

58

Name _____

Find the words on Silly Sea Serpent. Write them on the lines below.

1 _____

2 _____

3 _____

4 _____

5 _____

6 _____

Start here

c o t

o

t

d o t

g

t

o

h

o t

n

o t

l

o t

59

Name _____

Write each word three times.

d o g

f o g

h o g

j o g

l o g

60

Unscramble the words.

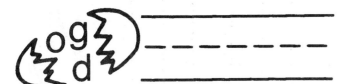
_____
_____

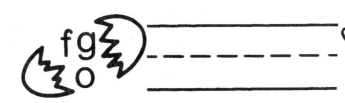
_____
_____

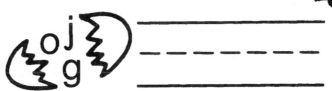
_____
_____

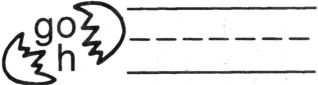
_____
_____

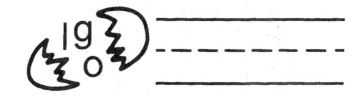
_____
_____

Now draw pictures of these words.

dog	hog	log

Name _____

Help Otto Octopus make words.

1 _____

2 _____

3 _____

4 _____

5 _____

Hi kids!

og

d l j h f

Color the rhyming fish.

fog   dog   pod   jog

job   log   mop   hog   not

62

Name _____

Find the words on Silly Sea Serpent. Write them on the lines below.

1 _____

2 _____

3 _____

4 _____

5 _____

Start here

FS-32054 Phonics Basics

Name _____

Write the word that goes with each picture. Use the word bank.

pop	hop	mop	top
hot	dot	cot	pot
dog	jog	fog	log

_____ _____ _____

_____ _____ _____

_____ _____ _____

Write the words you did not use here.

_____ _____ _____

_____ _____ _____

_____ _____ _____

                   FS-32054 Phonics Basics

Draw the picture.

cop with a mop	**dot on a dog**	**jog in the fog**
hot dog	**hog on a cot**	**hop over the log**
pot with a top	**dot on a pot**	**dog on a log**

FS-32054 Phonics Basics

Name _____

Finish the word in the boat with the correct letter.
Then write the word.

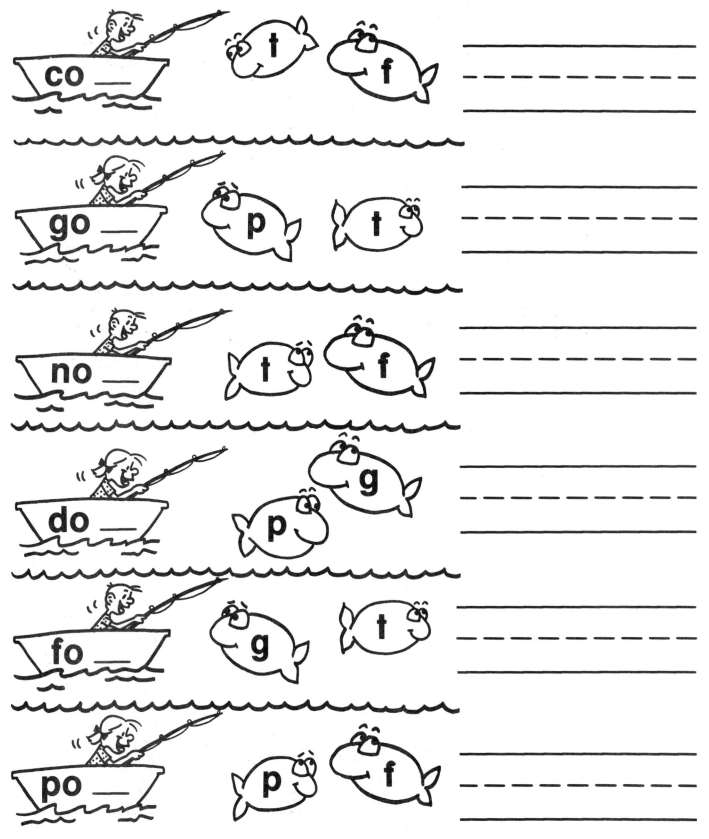

66

Choose words to put in the sentences.

The _____ has a _____ .

The _____ can _____ .

The _____ has no _____ .

My _____ is on the _____ .

jog	mop	cot	hog	top	pot	cop	dog

FS-32054 Phonics Basics

Name _____

Write six words that rhyme and...one more if you can!

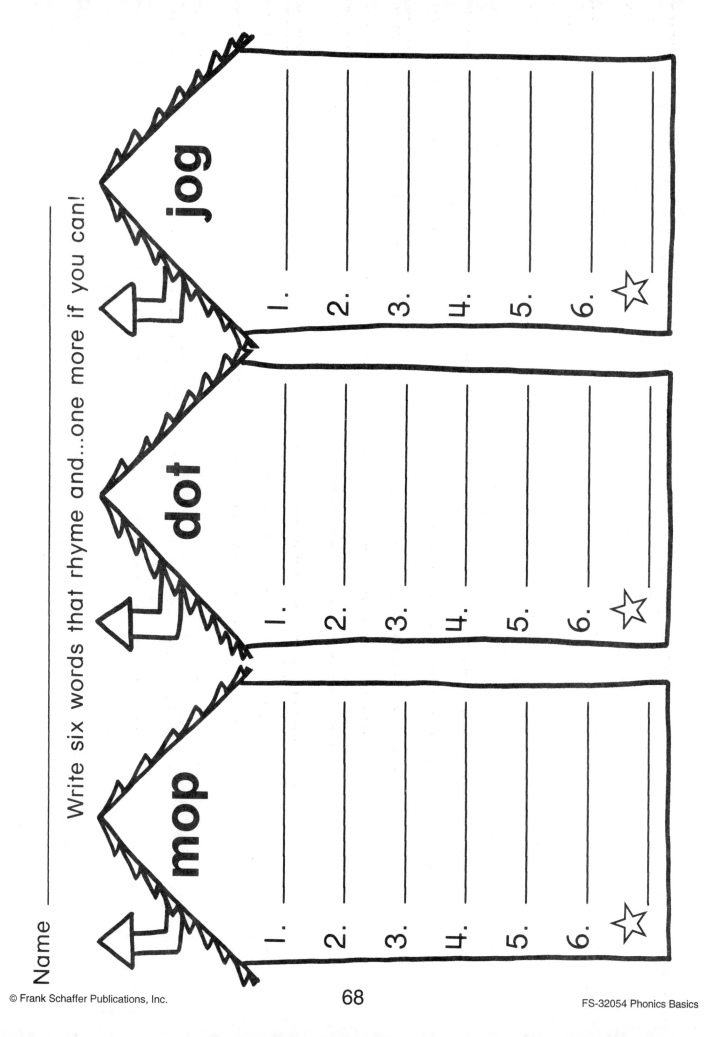

jog

1.
2.
3.
4.
5.
6.
☆

dot

1.
2.
3.
4.
5.
6.
☆

mop

1.
2.
3.
4.
5.
6.
☆

FS-32054 Phonics Basics

Name _____

Write each word three times.

bun

fun

run

sun

nun

Name _____

Unscramble the words.

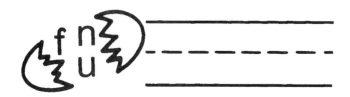

_____

_____

_____

_____

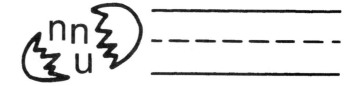

_____

_____

_____

_____

Now draw pictures of these words.

nun	sun	bun

FS-32054 Phonics Basics

Name _____

Help Otto Octopus make words.

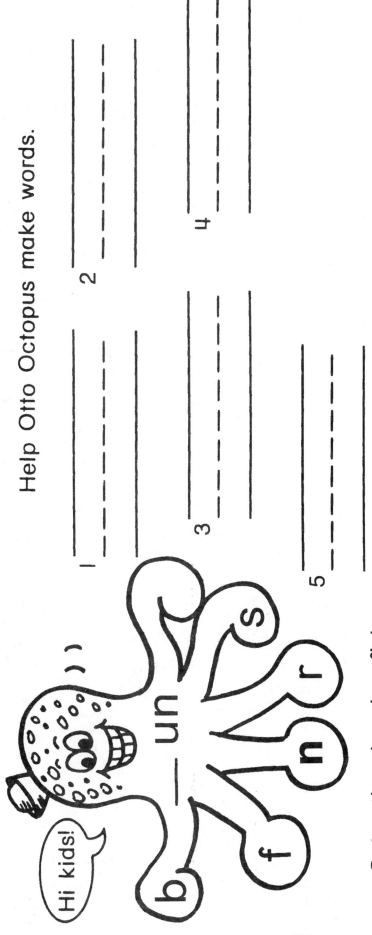

Hi kids!

1 _____

2 _____

3 _____

4 _____

5 _____

Color the rhyming fish.

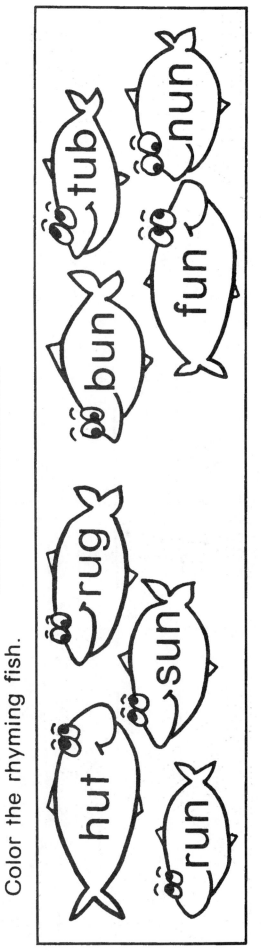

71

Name _____

Find the words on Silly Sea Serpent. Write them on the lines below.

1 _____

2 _____

3 _____

4 _____

5 _____

— un words

Start here

72

Name _____

Write each word three times.

bug

gug

hug

mug

rug

tug

73

Name _____

Unscramble the words.

ub g _____

gu d _____

hg u _____

u j g _____

u r g _____

gu t _____

Now draw pictures of these words.

bug	jug	tug

FS-32054 Phonics Basics

Name _____

Help Otto Octopus make words.

Hi kids!

ug
t
r
m
h
d
b

1 _____
2 _____
3 _____
4 _____
5 _____
6 _____

Color the rhyming fish.

rug

cut

sub

mug

bug

hug

tug

dug

sun

© Frank Schaffer Publications, Inc.

FS-32054 Phonics Basics

Name _____

Find the words on Silly Sea Serpent. Write them on the lines below.

1 _____

2 _____

3 _____

4 _____

5 _____

6 _____

Start here

FS-32054 Phonics Basics

Name _____

Write each word three times.

—ub words

cub

rub

sub

tub

hub

FS-32054 Phonics Basics

Name _____

Unscramble the words.

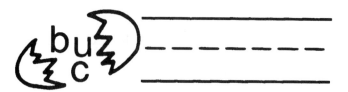

_____

- - - - - - - - - - - - - - -

_____

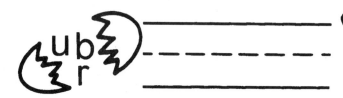

_____

- - - - - - - - - - - - - - -

_____

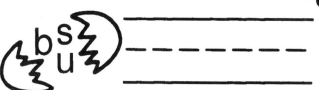

_____

- - - - - - - - - - - - - - -

_____

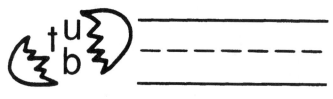

_____

- - - - - - - - - - - - - - -

_____

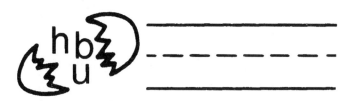

_____

- - - - - - - - - - - - - - -

_____

Now draw pictures of these words.

cub	sub	tub

Name _____

Help Otto Octopus make words.

1 _____

2 _____

3 _____

4 _____

5 _____

Hi kids!

ub

c   r   s   t   h

Color the rhyming fish.

cub fun cup tub sub hub cut bug rub

79

FS-32054 Phonics Basics

Name

Find the words on Silly Sea Serpent. Write them on the lines below.

1

2

3

4

5

Start here

FS-32054 Phonics Basics

Name _____

Write the word that goes with each picture. Use the word bank.

bun	jug	fun	sun
bug	cub	mug	rug
sub	tub	hug	hub

Write the words you did not use here.

_____   _____   _____

_____   _____   _____

FS-32054 Phonics Basics

Draw the picture.

sub in a bun	cub in a mug	bug in the sun
cub in the tub	bug with a jug	fun in the sun
run on the rug	sub in the tub	bug on the rug

FS-32054 Phonics Basics

Finish the word in the boat with the correct letter.
Then write the word.

bu ___   n   b   ----------

mu ___   g   n   ----------

fu ___   b   n   ----------

hu ___   n   g   ----------

tu ___   n   b   ----------

su ___   b   g   ----------

Name _____

Write six words that rhyme and...one more if you can!

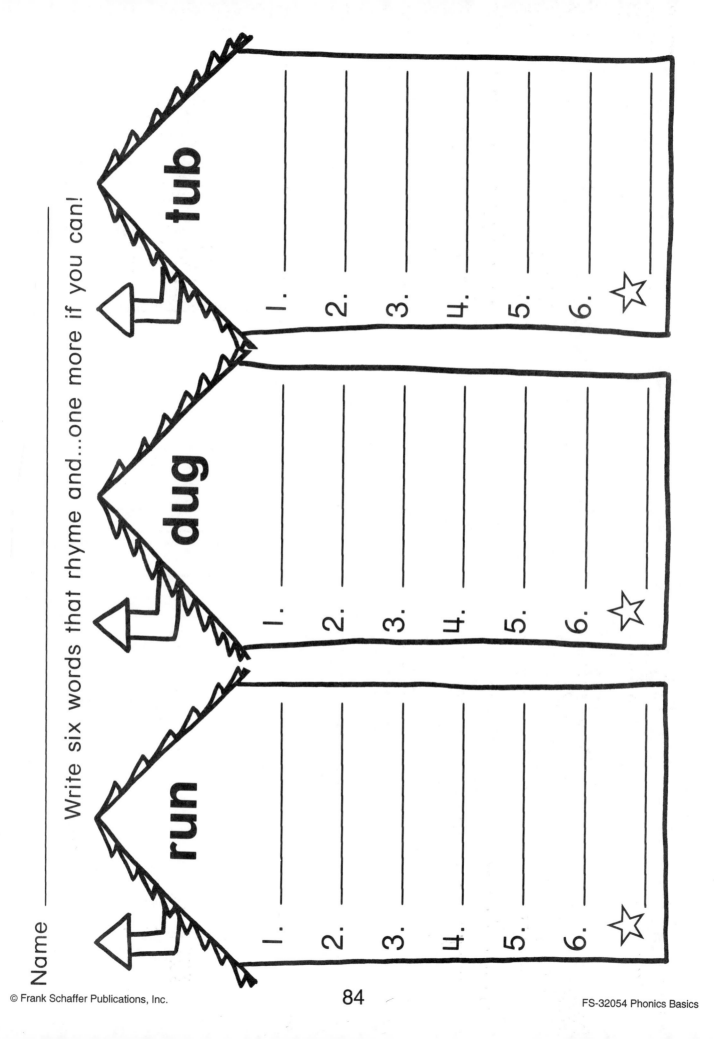

tub

1.
2.
3.
4.
5.
6.

dug

1.
2.
3.
4.
5.
6.

run

1.
2.
3.
4.
5.
6.

FS-32054 Phonics Basics

Name _____

cat	but	hat
cut	fan	hut
bat	fun	

Fill in the blanks with words.

1	I want to, _____ I can't.
2	I have a pet _____ .
3	That is a _____ .
4	Ow! I have a _____ .
5	Turn on the _____ .

Name _____

Fill in the blanks with words.

1 	These don't _____ .
2	I sat on a _____ !
3	I am so _____ .
4	I have a new _____ .
5	Spot is in my _____ .

FS-32054 Phonics Basics

Name _____

hot   dig   pop
hit   jog   pig
dog   big

Fill in the blanks with words.

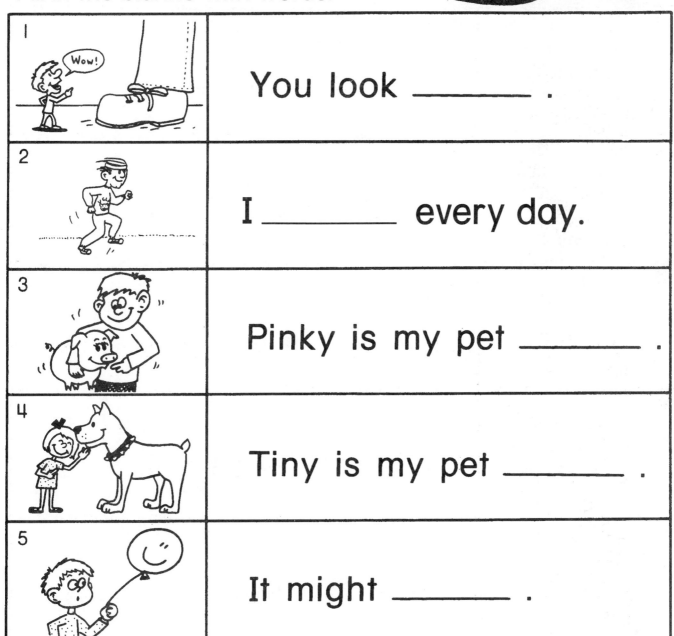

1	You look _____ .
2	I _____ every day.
3	Pinky is my pet _____ .
4	Tiny is my pet _____ .
5	It might _____ .

FS-32054 Phonics Basics

Name _____

not   sun   run
hug   dot   hop
top   bug

Fill in the blanks with words.

1	I _____ fast!
2	I am _____ a boy.
3	I love the _____ .
4	Mom gave me a _____ .
5	See my new _____ !

FS-32054 Phonics Basics

Name _____

name   came   like
game   time   bike
same   dime

Silent e

Fill in the blanks with words.

1 Ten cents, please.	It costs one _____ .
2	What _____ is it?
3 I'm Polly	What is your _____ ?
4 Good idea.	Let's play a _____ .
5	You two look the _____ .

FS-32054 Phonics Basics

Name _____

Once upon a time...

Fill in the blanks with words.

1	Look at the _____.
2	Don't _____ the door!
3	A red light means _____.
4	This is my new _____.
5	The peel made her _____.

Name _____

stir   snap   skip

stab   snug   skin

snip   snow

Fill in the blanks with words.

1	I love the _____.
2	_____ the batter.
3	I am _____ in bed.
4	_____ a small piece off.
5	We like to _____ .

FS-32054 Phonics Basics

Name _____

clip   club   crib
clap   claw   crow
clam   crab

Fill in the blanks with words.

1	Suzy is in her _____.
2	Look at that _____.
3	I _____ Max every month.
4	I found a _____.
5	Here is a _____ shell.

92

Name _____

These look tricky!

Fill in the blanks with words.

1	Beat the _____.
2	See the faucet _____.
3	Don't _____.
4	It's full to the _____.
5	I put on a _____ of paste.

I'm great.

Name _____

flag	frog	trip
flat	from	trim
flap	trap	

Fill in the blanks with words.

1 *Like this!*	Now _____ your wings.
2	Look out for the _____!
3	It's a letter _____ Grandma!
4 *Slow down!*	Look out for a _____.
5	This is our school_____.

FS-32054 Phonics Basics

Name _____

Fill in the blanks with words.

1	Let's _____ tag.
2	I will eat this _____.
3	Please_____ it in.
4	Look at that cat _____.
5	I am _____ you are here.

Name _____

wish	ship	shop
fish	shell	push
dish	wash	

Practice!

Fill in the blanks with words.

1	Here is your _____ of milk.
2	I caught a _____!
3	I _____ I had a brother.
4	What a pretty _____.
5	I got Rover at the pet _____.

Name _____

rich	chat path
chip	bath thin
chug	math

Fill in the blanks with words.

1	I'm taking a _____.
2	Let's _____.
3	I love to do _____.
4	I ate a potato _____.
5	I am not _____.

FS-32054 Phonics Basics

Name _____

sing   ring   song
wing   bang   long
king   hang

Fill in the blanks with words.

1	We like to _____ .
2	His nose is _____ .
3	I am the_____ .
4	I like your _____ .
5	She likes to _____ .

FS-32054 Phonics Basics

back   tack   lick
pack   pick   sick
sack   kick

More words!

Fill in the blanks with words.

1	Have a _____, Pooch.
2	I feel _____.
3	I _____ this one.
4	I have a _____ of gum.
5	What is in the _____ ?

FS-32054 Phonics Basics

look   took   wood

cook   hook   hood

book   good

Fill in the blanks with words.

1	Dad is a good _____ !
2	This is a great _____ !
3	Who _____ my pie?
4	_____ at the bird!
5	This smells _____ !

FS-32054 Phonics Basics

Name _____

tail   nail   rain
jail   mail   pain
fail   pail

Fill in the blanks with words.

1	I love the _____.
2	See my fuzzy _____?
3	Fill the _____ with sand.
4	Here is your _____.
5	Hammer that _____.

FS-32054 Phonics Basics

Name _____

coat	loan	road
boat	foam	load
goat	roam	

These look hard!

Fill in the blanks with words.

1	I have a toy _____.
2 Looks big.	This is a _____.
3 It's new.	I have a warm _____.
4	This is shaving _____.
5 ...for one week. Thanks.	I will _____ my bike to you.

FS-32054 Phonics Basics

Name _____

low	cow	pow
row	how	wow
tow	now	

Look! The first three words sound different!

Fill in the blanks with words.

1	Ginger is my _____.
2	Please show me _____.
3	_____ the boat.
4	We had to _____ the car.
5	Look on the _____ shelf.

FS-32054 Phonics Basics

Name _____

boy	pay	way
toy	day	may
joy	hay	

Fill in the blanks with words.

1	See my new _____!
2	I am a _____.
3	Have a nice _____.
4	I eat _____ sometimes.
5	I will _____ five cents.

FS-32054 Phonics Basics

Answer Key

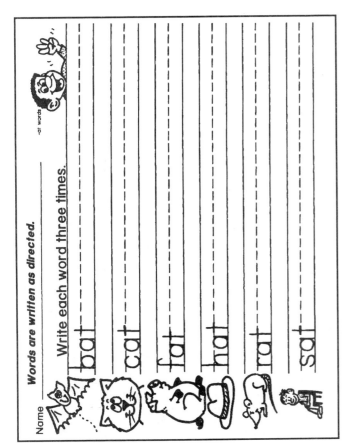

Page 1

Page 2

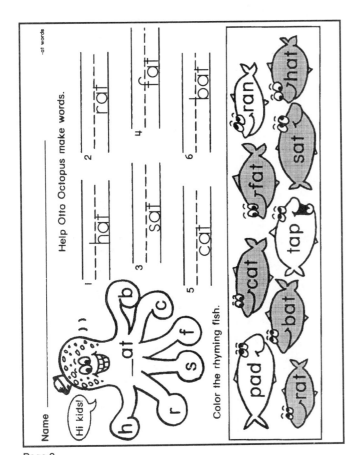

Page 3

Page 4

FS-32054 Phonics Basics

Answer Key

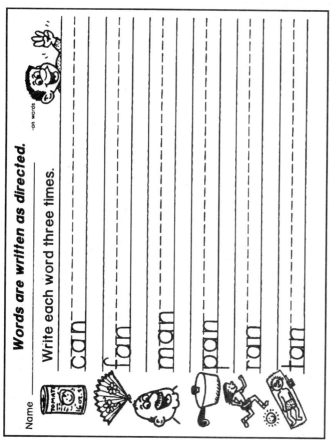

Page 5

Page 6

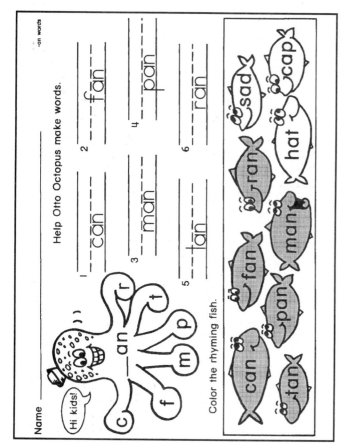

Page 7

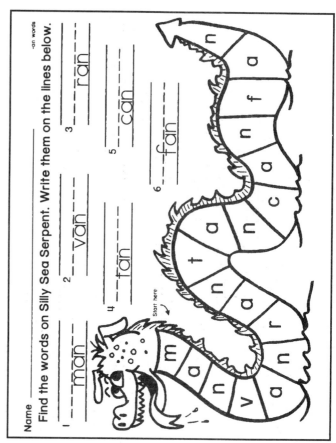

Page 8

106

Answer Key

Page 9

Page 10

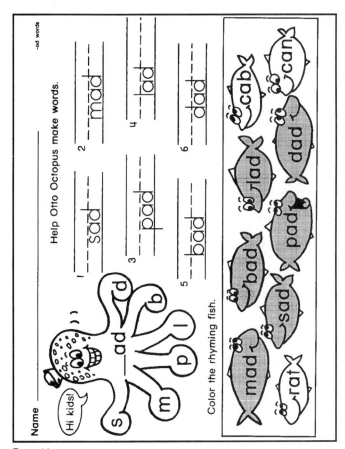

Page 11

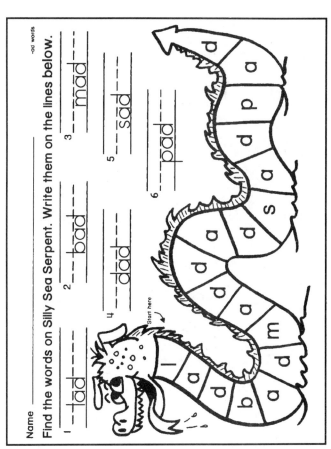

Page 12

Answer Key

Write the word that goes with each picture. Use the word bank.

can	fan	man	pan
bat	mad	cat	pad
hat	rat	dad	tan

p a n   f a n   b a t

h a t   m a n   c a t

r a t   m a d   c a n

Write the words you did not use here.

dad   pad   fan

Page 13

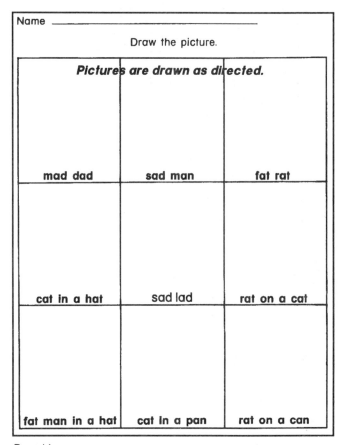

Draw the picture.

Pictures are drawn as directed.		
mad dad	sad man	fat rat
cat in a hat	sad lad	rat on a cat
fat man in a hat	cat in a pan	rat on a can

Page 14

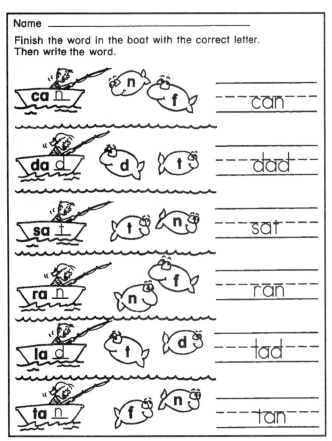

Finish the word in the boat with the correct letter.
Then write the word.

ca n   can

da d   dad

sa t   sat

ra n   ran

la d   lad

ta n   tan

Page 15

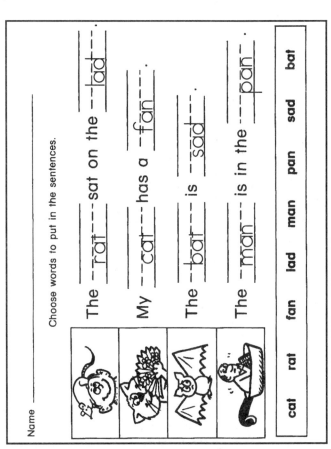

Choose words to put in the sentences.

The rat sat on the lad.

My cat has a fan.

The bat is sad.

The man is in the pan.

cat	rat	fan	lad	man	pan	sad	bat

Name _____

Page 16

Answer Key

109

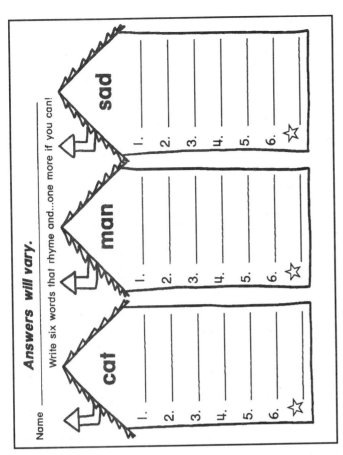

Page 17

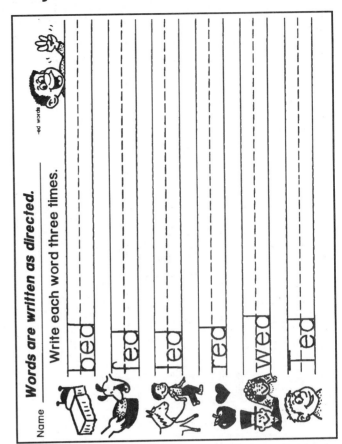

Page 18

Page 19

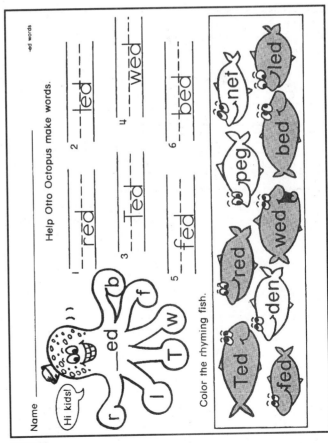

Page 20

Answer Key

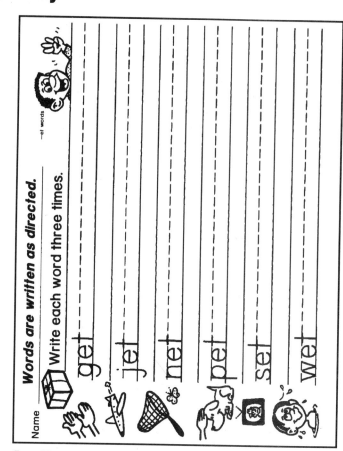

Page 21

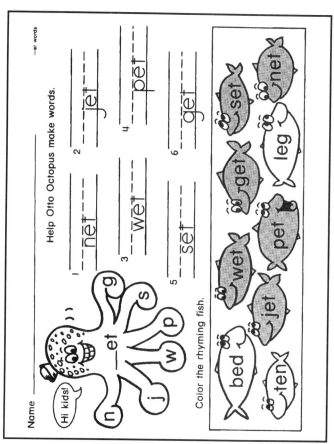

Page 22

Page 23

Page 24

110

Answer Key

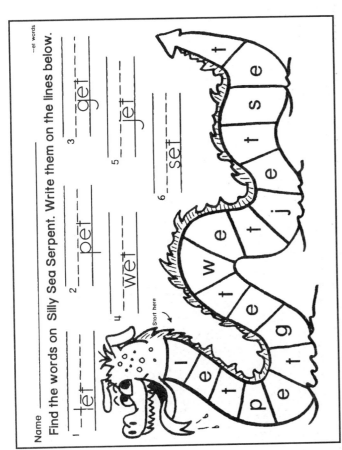

—et words

Name _____

Find the words on Silly Sea Serpent. Write them on the lines below.

1. __tet__   2. __pet__   3. __get__

4. __wet__   5. __set__   6. __jet__

Start here

Page 25

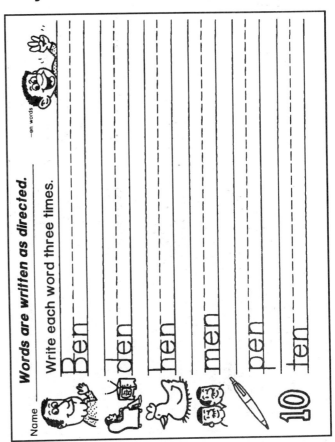

—en words

Name _____

Words are written as directed.

Write each word three times.

Ben

den

hen

men

pen

10 ten

Page 26

Name _____

—en words

Unscramble the words.

nhe → hen

enp → pen

edn → den

neB → Ben

neK → Ken

nem → men

Now draw pictures of these words.

hen	pen	den

Page 27

© Frank Schaffer Publications, Inc.

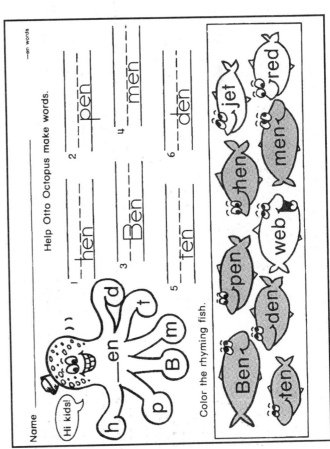

—en words

Name _____

Help Otto Octopus make words.

Hi kids!

h e n d t B m p

1. __hen__   2. __pen__

3. __Ben__   4. __men__

5. __ten__   6. __den__

Color the rhyming fish.

jet red hen men pen web den Ben ten

Page 28

111

FS-32054 Phonics Basics

Answer Key

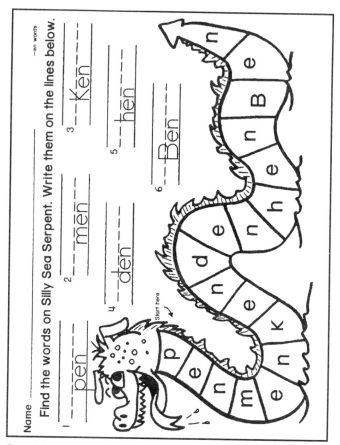

Name _____

Write the word that goes with each picture. Use the word bank.

jet	bed	get	net
Ted	pet	hen	men
pen	ten	red	wet

Write the words you did not use here.

get   red   wet

Name _____

Draw the picture.

Pictures are drawn as directed.		
red pen	bed on a jet	hen in a net
wet hen	ten men	Ted and Ben
pet in a pen	ten wet men	Ben's den

Name _____

Finish the word in the boat with the correct letter.
Then write the word.

fe **d**   **d**   **n**   fed

ne **t**   **n**   **t**   net

se **t**   **t**   **d**   set

te **n**   **n**   **t**   ten

je **t**   **d**   **t**   jet

ge **t**   **t**   **n**   get

112

Answer Key

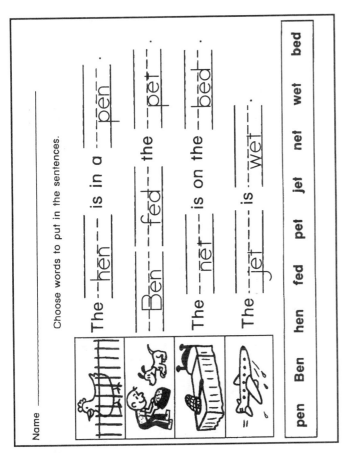

Page 33

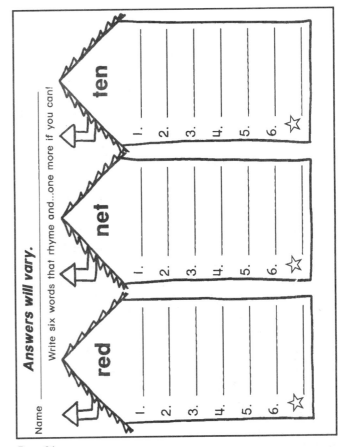

Page 34

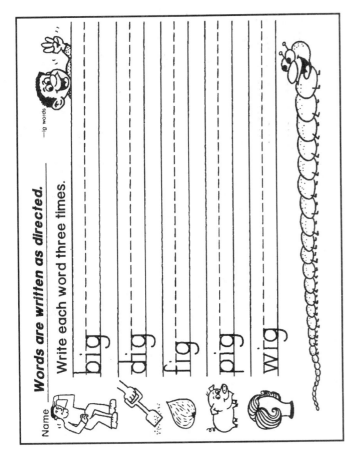

Page 35

Page 36

FS-32054 Phonics Basics

Answer Key

Page 37

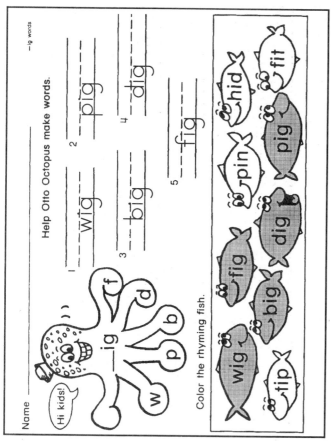

Name _____

—ig words

Hi kids!

ig

Help Otto Octopus make words.

1 ___ wig

2 ___ pig

3 ___ big

4 ___ dig

5 ___ fig

Color the rhyming fish.

Page 38

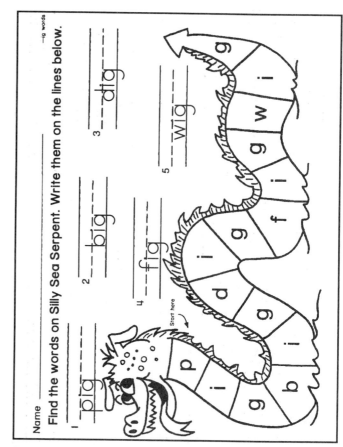

Name _____

—ig words

Find the words on Silly Sea Serpent. Write them on the lines below.

1 ___ pig

2 ___ big

3 ___ dig

4 ___ fig

5 ___ wig

Start here

Page 39

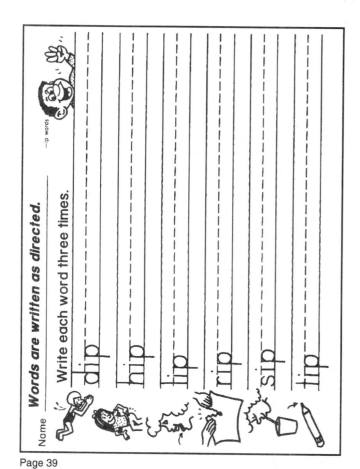

Name _____

—ip words

Words are written as directed.

Write each word three times.

dip

hip

lip

rip

sip

tip

Page 40

Name _____

—ip words

Unscramble the words.

p h i → hip

p i r → rip

i s p → sip

p i d → dip

i l p → lip

i p z → zip

Now draw pictures of these words.

lip	rip	hip

FS-32054 Basic Phonics

Answer Key

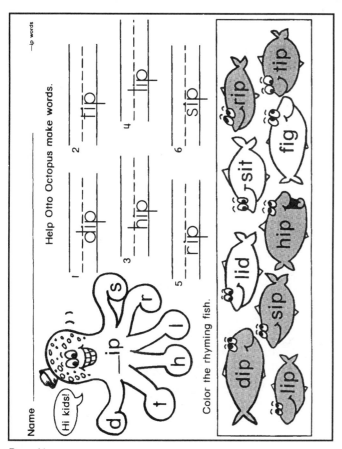

Page 41

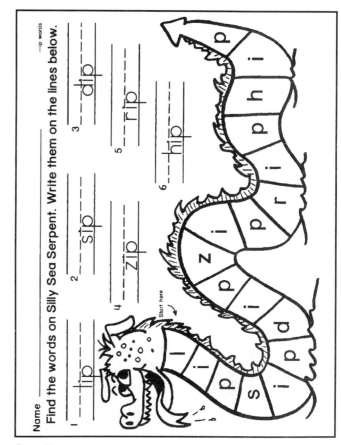

Page 42

Page 43

Page 44

Answer Key

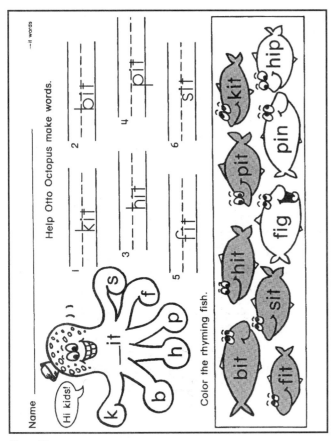

Page 45

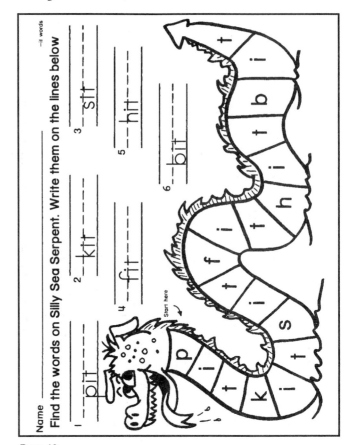

Page 46

Page 47

Name _____

Draw the picture.

Pictures are drawn as directed.		
big pig	pig with a big lip	pig in a pit
pig with a fig	Sue bit a fig.	pig with a wig

Page 48

Answer Key

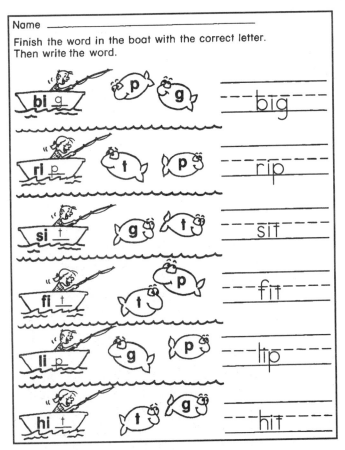

Name _____

Finish the word in the boat with the correct letter.
Then write the word.

bi **g** — big
ri **p** — rip
si **t** — sit
fi **t** — fit
li **p** — lip
hi **t** — hit

Page 49

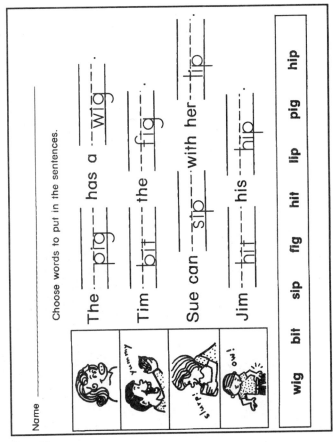

Name _____

Choose words to put in the sentences.

The **pig** has a **wig**.

Tim **bit** the **fig**.

Sue can **sip** with her **lip**.

Jim **hit** his **hip**.

wig   bit   sip   fig   hit   lip   pig   hip

Page 50

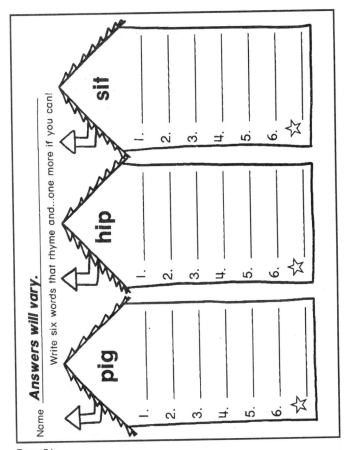

Name _____

Answers will vary.

Write six words that rhyme and...one more if you can!

pig 1. 2. 3. 4. 5. 6. ☆
hip 1. 2. 3. 4. 5. 6. ☆
sit 1. 2. 3. 4. 5. 6. ☆

Page 51

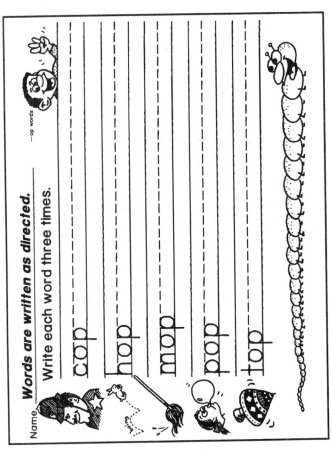

Name _____

Words are written as directed.

Write each word three times.

—op words

cop
hop
mop
pop
top

Page 52

117

© Frank Schaffer Publications, Inc.

FS-32054 Phonics Basics

Answer Key

Page 53

Name _____ —op words

Unscramble the words.

cop

hop

mop

pop

top

Now draw pictures of these words.

top	mop	hop

Page 53

Page 54

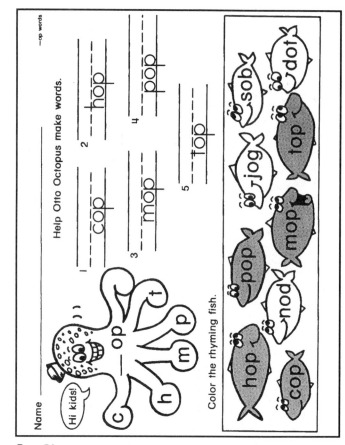

—op words

Name _____

Help Otto Octopus make words.

Hi kids!

1. cop
2. hop
3. mop
4. pop
5. top

Color the rhyming fish.

sob   dot   jog   top   pop   mop   nod   hop   cop

Page 54

Page 55

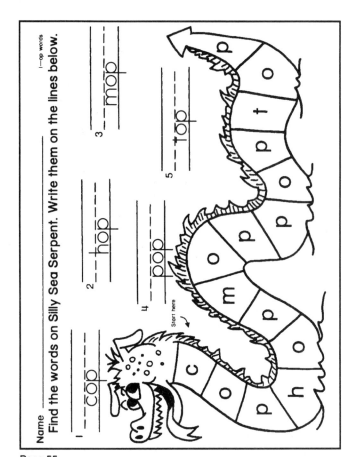

—op words

Name _____

Find the words on Silly Sea Serpent. Write them on the lines below.

1. cop
2. hop
3. mop
4. pop
5. top

Start here

Page 55

Page 56

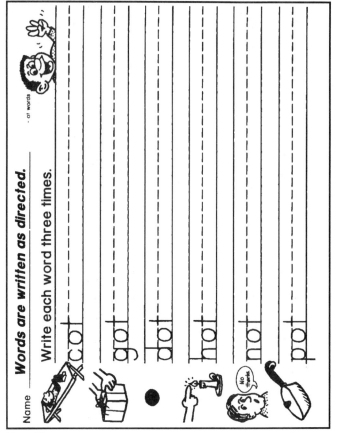

— ot words

Name _____

Words are written as directed.

Write each word three times.

cot

got

dot

hot

not

pot

Page 56

FS-32054 Phonics Basics

Answer Key

Unscramble the words.

—ot words

cot

dot

got

hot

not

lot

Now draw pictures of these words.

dot	cot	hot

Page 57

—ot words

Help Otto Octopus make words.

Hi kids!

1 cot
2 dot
3 got
4 hot
5 not
6 pot

Color the rhyming fish.

fog   cot

not   pot

dot   rod

got

hot   pop

Page 58

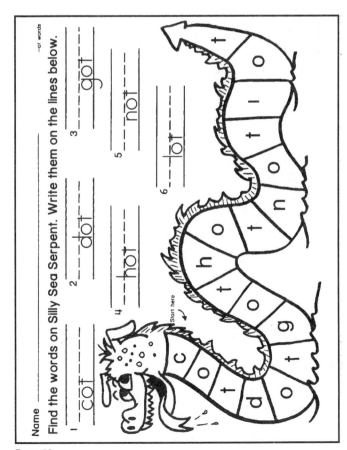

—ot words

Find the words on Silly Sea Serpent. Write them on the lines below.

1 cot
2 dot
3 got
4 hot
5 not
6 lot

Start here

Page 59

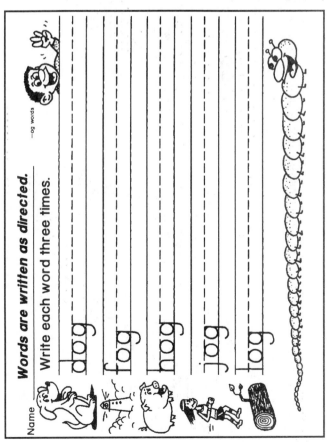

Words are written as directed.

—og words

Write each word three times.

dog

fog

hog

jog

log

Page 60

© Frank Schaffer Publications, Inc.

119

FS-32054 Phonics Basics

Answer Key

Page 61

Name _____ —og words

Unscramble the words.

og d → dog

fg o → fog

oj g → jog

go h → hog

lg o → log

Now draw pictures of these words.

| dog | hog | log |

Page 61

Page 62

Name _____ —og words

Help Otto Octopus make words.

Hi kids!

1. dog
2. fog
3. hog
4. fog
5. hog

Color the rhyming fish.

fog job dog log pod mop hog jog not

Page 62

Page 63

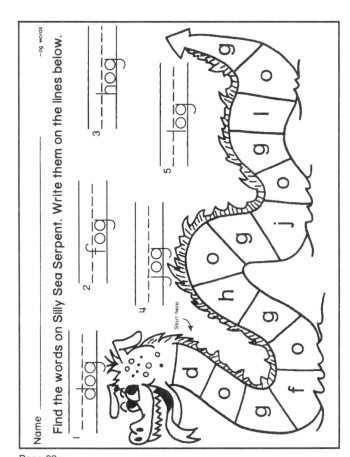

Name _____ —og words

Find the words on Silly Sea Serpent. Write them on the lines below.

Start here

1. dog
2. fog
3. hog
4. jog
5. log

Page 63

Page 64

Name _____

Write the word that goes with each picture. Use the word bank.

pop	hop	mop	top
hot	dot	cot	pot
dog	jog	fog	log

p o t   m o p   d o g

h o p   t o p   l o g

c o t   j o g   d o t

Write the words you did not use here.

pop   hot   fog

Page 64

Answer Key

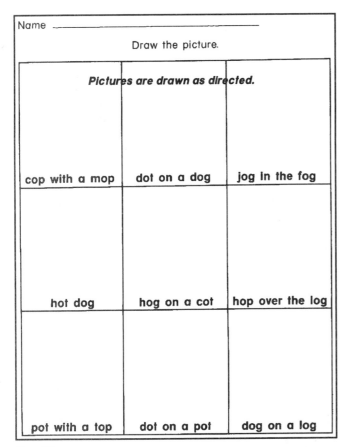

Name _____

Draw the picture.

Pictures are drawn as directed.		
cop with a mop	dot on a dog	jog in the fog
hot dog	hog on a cot	hop over the log
pot with a top	dot on a pot	dog on a log

Page 65

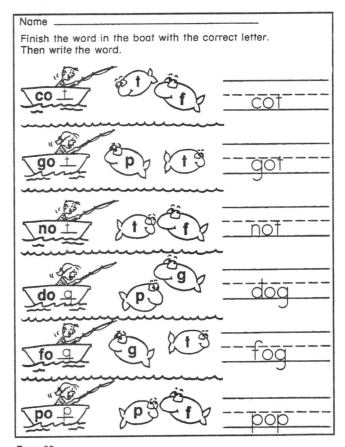

Name _____

Finish the word in the boat with the correct letter.
Then write the word.

co_   t   f   cot

go_   p   t   got

no_   t   f   not

do_   p   g   dog

fo_   g   t   fog

po_   p   f   pop

Page 66

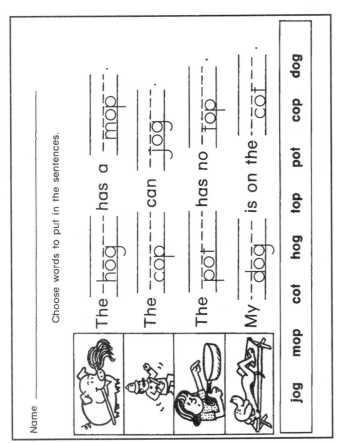

Name _____

Choose words to put in the sentences.

The hog has a mop.

The cop can jog.

The pot has no top.

My dog is on the cot.

jog   mop   cot   hog   top   pot   cop   dog

Page 67

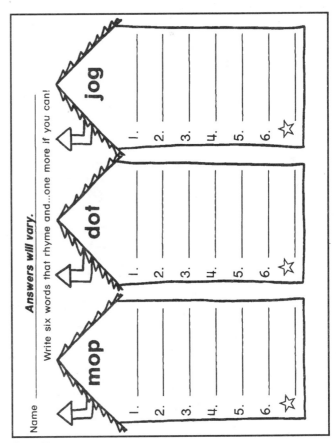

Name _____

Write six words that rhyme and...one more if you can!

Answers will vary.

jog
1. 2. 3. 4. 5. 6. ☆

dot
1. 2. 3. 4. 5. 6. ☆

mop
1. 2. 3. 4. 5. 6. ☆

Page 68

© Frank Schaffer Publications, Inc.

121

FS-32054 Phonics Basics

Answer Key

Page 69

Page 70

Page 71

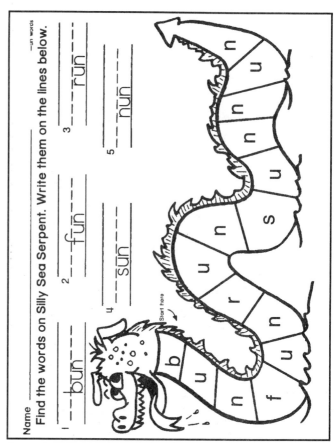

Page 72

122

Answer Key

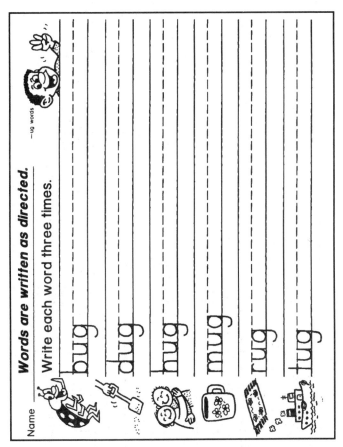

Words are written as directed.

Write each word three times.

bug
dug
hug
mug
rug
tug

Page 73

Name _____

Name _____   —ug words

Unscramble the words.

ub g → bug
gu d → dug
hg u → hug
u j g → jug
ur g → rug
gu t → tug

Now draw pictures of these words.

| bug | jug | tug |

Page 74

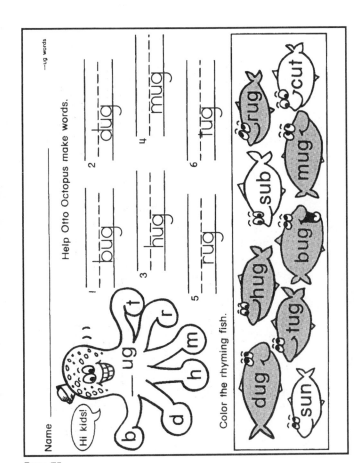

Name _____   —ug words

Help Otto Octopus make words.

1. bug
2. dug
3. hug
4. mug
5. rug
6. tug

Hi kids!

Color the rhyming fish.

rug   cut
sub   mug
hug   bug
tug   fish
dug   sun

Page 75

Name _____   —ug words

Find the words on Silly Sea Serpent. Write them on the lines below.

1. bug
2. dug
3. hug
4. jug
5. rug
6. tug

Start here

Page 76

123

© Frank Schaffer Publications, Inc.

FS-32054 Phonics Basics

Answer Key

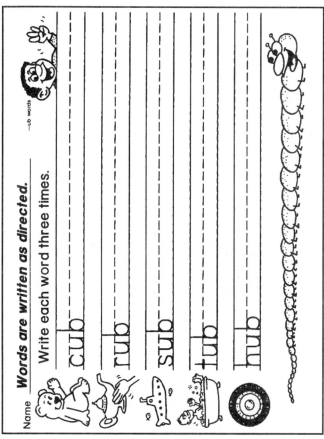

Words are written as directed.

Name _____

Write each word three times.

cub

rub

sub

tub

hub

Page 77

Name _____

Unscramble the words.

cub

rub

sub

tub

hub

Now draw pictures of these words.

cub	sub	tub

Page 78

Name _____

Help Otto Octopus make words.

Hi kids!

1 cub   2 rub

3 sub   4 tub

5 hub

Color the rhyming fish.

cub   cup   fun   tub   hub   sub   cut   bug   rub

Page 79

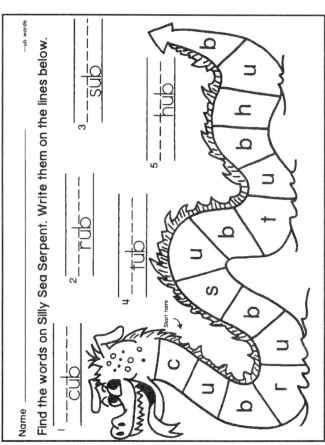

Name _____

Find the words on Silly Sea Serpent. Write them on the lines below.

1 cub   2 rub   3 sub

4 tub   5 hub

Start here

Page 80

Answer Key

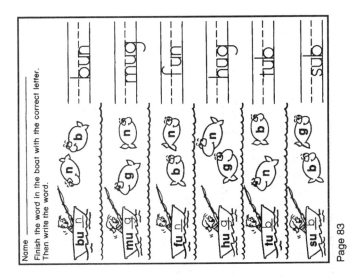

Page 83

Name _____
Finish the word in the boat with the correct letter. Then write the word.

bun — mug — fun — hug — tub — sub

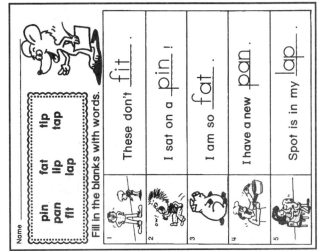

Page 86

Name _____

pin	fat	tip
pan	lip	tap
fit		

Fill in the blanks with words.

1. These don't **fit**.
2. I sat on a **pin**!
3. I am so **fat**.
4. I have a new **pan**.
5. Spot is in my **lap**.

Name _____
Draw the picture.

Pictures are drawn as directed.

sub in a bun	cub in a mug	bug in the sun
cub in the tub	bug with a jug	fun in the sun
run on the rug	sub in the tub	bug on the rug

Page 82

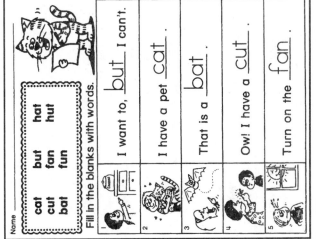

Page 85

Name _____

cat	but	hat
cut	fan	hut
bat	fun	

Fill in the blanks with words.

1. I want to, **but** I can't.
2. I have a pet **cat**.
3. That is a **bat**.
4. Ow! I have a **cut**.
5. Turn on the **fan**.

Name _____
Write the word that goes with each picture. Use the word bank.

bun	jug	fun	sun
bug	cub	mug	rug
sub	tub	hug	hub

mug — cub — tub
bun — sub — sun
rug — jug — bug

Write the words you did not use here.

fun — hug — hub

Page 81

Name _____
Answers will vary.

Write six words that rhyme and...one more if you can!

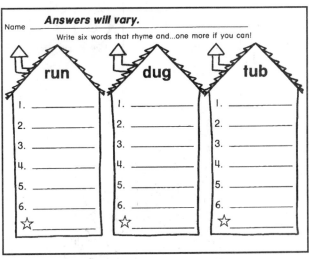

run | **dug** | **tub**

1. ___ 2. ___ 3. ___ 4. ___ 5. ___ 6. ___ ☆

Page 84

FS-32054 Phonics Basics

Answer Key

Name _____

Silent e

name came like bike
game time dime same

Fill in the blanks with words.

1. It costs one dime.
2. What time is it?
3. What is your name?
4. Let's play a game.
5. You two look the same.

Page 89

Name _____

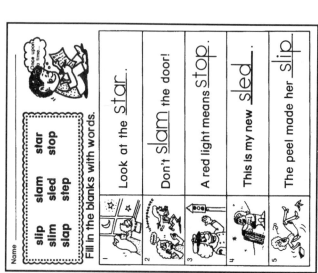

clip club crib crow
clap claw
clam crab

Fill in the blanks with words.

1. Suzy is in her crib.
2. Look at that crow.
3. I clip Max every month.
4. I found a crab.
5. Here is a clam shell.

Page 92

Name _____

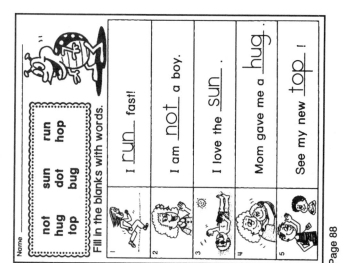

not sun run hop
hug dot
top bug

Fill in the blanks with words.

1. I run fast!
2. I am not a boy.
3. I love the sun.
4. Mom gave me a hug.
5. See my new top!

Page 88

Name _____

stir snap skip skin
stab snug
snip snow

Fill in the blanks with words.

1. I love the snow.
2. Stir the batter.
3. I am snug in bed.
4. Snip a small piece off.
5. We like to skip.

Page 91

Name _____

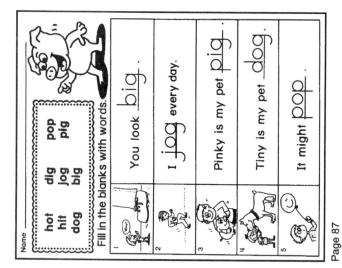

hot dig pop pig
hit jog
dog big

Fill in the blanks with words.

1. You look big.
2. I jog every day.
3. Pinky is my pet pig.
4. Tiny is my pet dog.
5. It might pop.

Page 87

Name _____

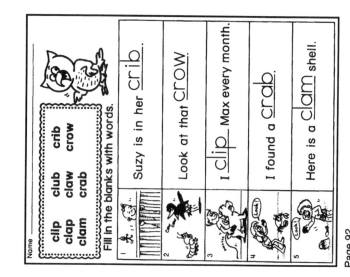

slip slam star stop
slim sled
slap step

Fill in the blanks with words.

1. Look at the star.
2. Don't slam the door!
3. A red light means stop.
4. This is my new sled.
5. The peel made her slip.

Page 90

126

Answer Key

grin glad play
grip glow plum
grab plug

Fill in the blanks with words.

1. Let's <u>play</u> tag.
2. I will eat this <u>plum</u>.
3. Please <u>plug</u> it in.
4. Look at that cat <u>grin</u>.
5. I am <u>glad</u> you are here.

Page 95

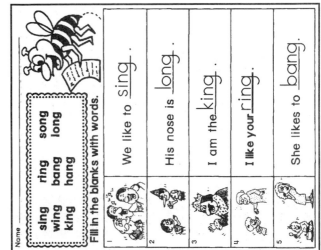

sing ring song
wing bang long
king hang

Fill in the blanks with words.

1. We like to <u>sing</u>.
2. His nose is <u>long</u>.
3. I am the <u>king</u>.
4. I like your <u>ring</u>.
5. She likes to <u>bang</u>.

Page 98

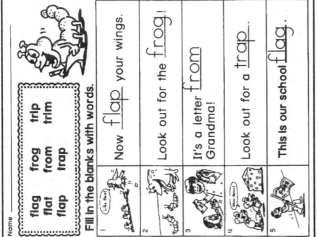

flag frog trip
flat from trim
flap trap

Fill in the blanks with words.

1. Now <u>flap</u> your wings.
2. Look out for the <u>frog</u>!
3. It's a letter <u>from</u> Grandma!
4. Look out for a <u>trap</u>.
5. This is our school <u>flag</u>.

Page 94

rich chat path
chip bath thin
chug math

Fill in the blanks with words.

1. I'm taking a <u>bath</u>.
2. Let's <u>chat</u>.
3. I love to do <u>math</u>.
4. I ate a potato <u>chip</u>.
5. I am not <u>thin</u>.

Page 97

brag blow drip
brim drum drag
blob drop

Fill in the blanks with words.

1. Beat the <u>drum</u>.
2. See the faucet <u>drip</u>.
3. Don't <u>brag</u>.
4. It's full to the <u>brim</u>.
5. I put on a <u>blob</u> of paste.

Page 93

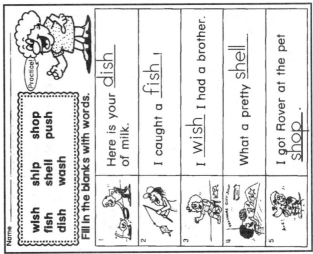

wish ship shop
fish shell push
dish wash

Fill in the blanks with words.

1. Here is your <u>dish</u> of milk.
2. I caught a <u>fish</u>!
3. I <u>wish</u> I had a brother.
4. What a pretty <u>shell</u>.
5. I got Rover at the pet <u>shop</u>.

Page 96

Answer Key

Name

tail nail rain
jail mail pain
fail pail

Fill in the blanks with words.

1. I love the rain.
2. See my fuzzy tail?
3. Fill the pail with sand.
4. Here is your mail.
5. Hammer that nail.

Page 101

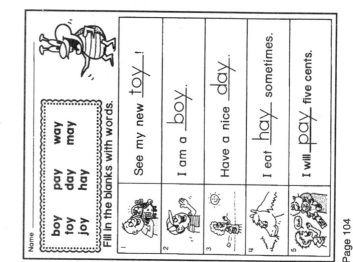

Name

boy pay way
toy day may
joy hay

Fill in the blanks with words.

1. See my new toy!
2. I am a boy.
3. Have a nice day.
4. I eat hay sometimes.
5. I will pay five cents.

Page 104

Name

look took wood
cook hook hood
book good

Fill in the blanks with words.

1. Dad is a good cook!
2. This is a great book!
3. Who took my pie?
4. Look at the bird!
5. This smells good!

Page 100

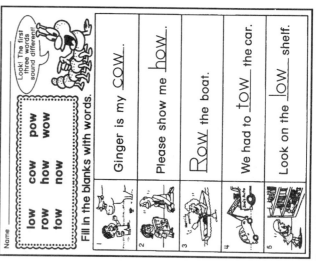

Look! The first three words sound different!

Name

low cow pow
row how wow
tow now

Fill in the blanks with words.

1. Ginger is my cow.
2. Please show me how.
3. Row the boat.
4. We had to tow the car.
5. Look on the low shelf.

Page 103

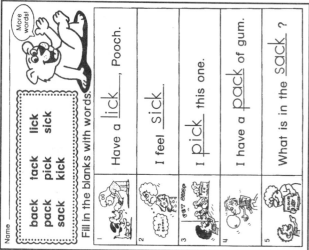

More words!

Name

back tack lick
pack pick sick
sack kick

Fill in the blanks with words.

1. Have a lick, Pooch.
2. I feel sick.
3. I pick this one.
4. I have a pack of gum.
5. What is in the sack?

Page 99

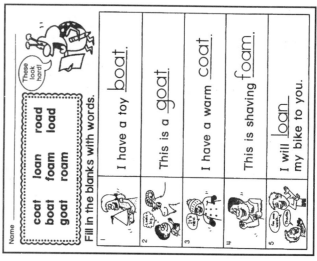

These look hard!

Name

coat loan road
boat foam load
goat roam

Fill in the blanks with words.

1. I have a toy boat!
2. This is a goat.
3. I have a warm coat.
4. This is shaving foam.
5. I will loan my bike to you.

Page 102

128